Louis Pasteur
Father of Modern Medicine

Beverley Birch

BLACKBIRCH PRESS, INC.
WOODBRIDGE, CONNECTICUT

Published by Blackbirch Press, Inc.
260 Amity Road
Woodbridge, CT 06525
Web site: http://www.blackbirch.com
e-mail: staff@blackbirch.com

© 2001 Blackbirch Press, Inc.
First U.S. Edition

First published in Great Britain as *Scientists Who Have Changed the World* by Exley Publications Ltd., Chalk Hill, Watford, 1990.
© Exley Publications, Ltd., 1990
© Beverley Birch, 1990

10 9 8 7 6 5 4 3 2 1

Photo Credits:
Anthony Blake Photo Library: 42; Bridgeman Art Library: 9, 34-35, 43; Giraudon: 19, 26; John Cleare: 4; Mary Evans Picture Library: 8, 41; Exley Photographic Library: Nick Birch 12 (left), 16 (below both), 30, 31 (above), 35 (below), 38, 57 (both); Giraudon: Musée des Beaux-Arts, Nantes 25; Georges Goldner: 16 (above), 58 (below), 59; Hulton-Deutsh Collection/CORBIS: front cover; Hulton Picture Library: 40 (above), 45, 51; Illustrated London News: 11; The Mansell Collection: 55; Oxford Scientific Films: G.I. Bernard 47 (all); Pasteur Institute: 5, 15, 36, 40 (below), 61; Roger-Viollet: 50, 56; Ann Ronan Picture Library: 21, 28, 29, 44, 46 (all), 49, 54, 58 (above); Science Photo Library: 7, 20, 31 (below), CNRI 53 (below), Eric Grave 12-13, 53 (above), David Scharf 23, Sinclair Stammers 22, John Walsh, 33, 39.

Printed in China

Library of Congress Cataloging-in-Publication Data
Birch, Beverley.
      Louis Pasteur : father of modern medicine / by Beverley Birch.
             p. cm. — (Giants of science)
Includes index.
      ISBN 1-56711-336-2
      1. Pasteur, Louis, 1822-1895—Juvenile literature. 2. Scientists—France—Biography—Juvenile literature. 3. Microbiologists—France—Biography—Juvenile literature. [1. Pasteur, Louis, 1822-1895. 2. Scientists. 3. Microbiologists.] I. Title. II. Series.
Q143.P2 M33 2001   00-012019
579' .092—dc21   CIP
                                                                   AC

JB
PASTEUR

Contents

Left: *Mont Blanc in the French Alps*

Right: *Louis Pasteur climbed Mont Blanc to test his theory that few germs would enter sterile flasks when he opened them in clean, mountain air.*

The Hunt for Pure Air

The procession wound its way up the mountain path. The guides moved ahead on the stony track. Behind them, a mule swayed beneath a load of strange, bulbous bottles. Near the mule, a small, eager-faced man with glasses scurried about, checking the mule's harness and guiding the animal along the edge of the precipice.

The group toiled up to the glistening peaks of snowy Mont Blanc. They breathed in the mountain air as they climbed in the morning sunshine. At last, they reached the white, untouched snows of Mer de Glace, the Sea of Ice.

Here, on an expanse of the glacier, a strange kind of ceremony began. The small man lit a lamp, which produced a powerful, jet-like flame. Carefully he removed a bottle from its cradle on the mule's back. It was not an ordinary bottle, but a plump, round-bellied glass flask with a narrow, straight neck that tapered to a point.

The man held it above his head. Inside the flask was a clear liquid that caught the light from snow and ice. With a pair of steel pincers, the man snapped off the tip of the flask's glass neck. If you had been close enough to him, you could have heard a sharp hiss of air rushing through the narrow opening into the belly of the flask. Almost immediately, the man took the lamp and ran its flame back and forth across the opening. The glass melted, sealing the opening shut.

5

The small man took a second flask, snapped its glass neck, listened for the faint hiss of air, and then quickly ran the flame back and forth across the opening. He repeated the procedure until twenty flasks had been opened and closed again.

Then the man's face relaxed, and he smiled. Success! It had worked this time. Yesterday, the group had failed.

The day before, everything had gone according to plan—until the moment the man had tried to seal the neck of the first flask with the lamp. The wind had whipped the flame in all directions. Against the brilliant sky and the glare of snow, Pasteur could not see the flame. There had been no hope of aiming it at the open neck of the flask.

There had only been one solution. The group had abandoned the task, retraced their steps, and found a person in the village of Chamonix at the foot of the mountain who could create a lamp that could give off a steady flame.

The Great Debate

What exactly was happening on that icy morning on Mont Blanc? Louis Pasteur had set out on a journey to prove that microorganisms are in the air. He set about conducting a precise and simple scientific experiment. Pasteur was going to settle, once and for all, this major question of science.

For weeks, Pasteur and his assistants had been preparing for the experiment. They had cleaned the flasks and made a liquid to put inside them. They had boiled the flasks, and then they had sealed them and packed them with great care. Some of the flasks had been carried across Paris and placed in cellars or dusty yards. Others had been hoisted up a hill near Pasteur's hometown of Arbois. Still others had gone by train to Chamonix, the starting point of their journey by mule on the path up the Alps to the pure air of Mont Blanc.

"I am the most hesitating of men, the most fearful of committing myself when I lack evidence. But on the contrary, no consideration can keep me from defending what I hold as true when I can rely on solid scientific evidence."

Louis Pasteur

When Louis Pasteur looked for solid proof of something, he left nothing to chance. "Always doubt yourself, till the facts cannot be doubted," Pasteur said.

Pasteur's own words are part of the key to his enormous contribution to the world. He believed in attention to the smallest of details, until there could be no question of any mistake.

There are various claims about exactly what constituted Pasteur's work. Some say he invented everything down to the smallest detail. Others credit him with single-handedly developing and proving the truth of the germ theory of diseases. This theory states that the germs of microscopic creatures known as microbes are the cause of many diseases. To argue the various claims obscures the importance of Pasteur's gigantic contribution to science and medicine.

Some of the scientific observations that Pasteur tackled had been around for a long time. Two hundred years earlier, the first microscope had revealed the vast world of tiny creatures that came to be known as microbes. Pasteur's observations were revolutionary enough to seem as if they were the first.

The Key to Understanding Diseases

Pasteur's research confirmed old theories and discovered new facts about microbes. Louis Pasteur also saw the interconnection between the information that already existed and theories he was exploring. Pasteur viewed microbes as the root of many life processes of the world. He supported his premise with painstaking experiments.

Pasteur theorized that microbes not only live and die, but they are also the key to understanding disease. Pasteur's vision changed the scientific world's perception of birth, life, decay, and the death of matter. With this perception, scientists were able to unlock the secrets of disease. Before Pasteur's discoveries, doctors could only help people to

This fifteenth-century German woodcut shows a man dying of the plague.

endure—and sometimes survive—disease. After Pasteur's discoveries, doctors began to cure and prevent illnesses.

In the decades following Pasteur's discoveries, new sciences were born. The first was the science of microbiology, the study of microscopic forms of life. Immunology, the scientific study of the immune system and causes, control and prevention of diseases also developed, through inoculation and immunization. These are the techniques that encourage the body to develop its own immunity to microbes. Doctors also started to use aseptic techniques, the practice of controlling and destroying germs in hospitals, particularly in surgery. Pasteur and those he trained were in the forefront of these great developments in science and medicine.

Pasteur's research and findings benefitted and affected many industries, including the manufacturing of wine and beer, the care of silkworms and the harvesting of silk, and diseases affecting cattle and sheep. In fact, these industries might not have survived without Pasteur's discoveries.

Right: *This illustration shows overcrowding and dirty food and water as ways in which epidemic diseases were spread.*

Opposite page: *Before treatments were available for cholera, people could die within six hours of falling ill. This painting of a mother and her child is by Henry Jules Jean Geoffroy, 1853–1924.*

Today, we all depend on pasteurization, the technique that bears Pasteur's name. Every day, dairies free our milk from disease-causing germs using this heat-based process.

Enemies of the Germ Theory

Not surprisingly, Louis Pasteur made enemies during his work—particularly as a standard-bearer of a new germ theory of disease that went against long-held theories. Many worked to find inconsistencies in his research and to discredit him. There were some inconsistencies, but they were few compared to the momentum Pasteur brought in advancing both science and medicine.

What was Pasteur trying to prove on Mont Blanc? It was a question that scientists had been arguing about for 100 years. Pasteur wanted to answer the question of whether there are germs in the air. It is hard now to think of this as a revolutionary idea because we accept the importance of using soaps and antiseptic cleaners; we clean and dress wounds; and doctors do their best to perform operations in germ-free conditions with germ-free instruments.

Now we know that there are microscopic living organisms on, and in, everything in the world—embedded in solid matter, floating in particles of airborne dust, and permeating water and other liquids. These microorganisms perform many essential tasks for us. They make waste materials decay to provide food for plant life. They turn raw materials into bread or wine. Some even take part in the digestive process in our bodies. We also now know that other microbes cause disease when they enter a human, animal, or plant body. These microorganisms can kill both people or animals.

One hundred years before Pasteur was born, Anton van Leeuwenhoek, a Dutchman, had

discovered the tiny creatures now known as microorganisms. Leeuwenhoek had an enormous curiosity about the world around him, and he had heard that a newly invented magnifying lens could help. Leeuwenhoek used the lens to look at human skin and hair, tree bark, seeds, insects, the cavities of rotten teeth—they all revealed their tiny secrets under the scrutiny of his lenses.

This illustration shows people burning fires of tar and sulfur in Granada in 1887. The fires were a vain attempt to disinfect the streets.

Leeuwenhoek and His Microscope

Leeuwenhoek had, in fact, invented what we now call the microscope. He is often called the "father of microbiology." From his quiet life in a small Dutch town, he changed the way people looked at the world. For the first time, people realized there was a world of creatures so tiny that they were invisible to the naked eye.

One day, as Leeuwenhoek was looking through one of his magnifying lenses, he was transfixed by the sight of millions of tiny creatures in the rainwater in

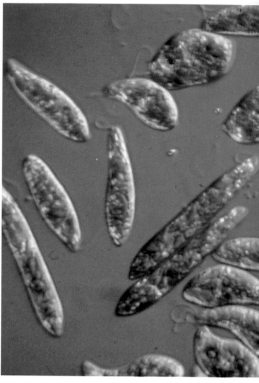

his yard! Leeuwenhoek compared the size of these animalcules (tiny animals), as he called them, to the size of the eye of a louse, which he had determined was very constant in size. The animalcules were 1,000 times smaller!

Leeuwenhoek made guesses as to what they were doing, but it never occurred to him that they were causing decay or disease. In his many observations, Leeuwenhoek discovered that the animalcules were killed by heat. One day, as he was squinting at scrapings from his own teeth, he found that after he'd drunk scalding hot coffee, the creatures were either dead or very sluggish.

Leeuwenhoek wrote down his findings and sent them to scientists in England who had recently formed the Royal Society in order to exchange scientific ideas with one another. Leeuwenhoek wrote that he could grow the one-celled creatures in water

mixed with pepper and that one drop of pepper-water held more than 2.7 million of them! The scientists in England built microscopes, repeated Leeuwenhoek's experiments, and verified that they were true.

Spallanzani's Work on Microbes

After the initial reaction to Leeuwenhoek's discoveries, his so-called animalcules were almost forgotten. Leeuwenhoek was long dead and the eighteenth century was well past the halfway mark when an Italian priest named Lazzaro Spallanzani, who was also a professor at the University of Reggio in Italy, became fascinated by the one-celled microscopic organisms.

In Spallanzani's time there was a great debate going on. The question was this: Does every living thing have to have parents, or can living things spring into life spontaneously?

Is There Spontaneous Life?

The popular idea in Spallanzani's day—and it remained so until well after Pasteur's death—was that things came alive spontaneously. People believed if you buried the carcass of a bull, a swarm of bees would pop out of the burial area spontaneously! Wasps and beetles would emerge out of dung, and maggots would spring from meat.

Spallanzani thought this idea was ridiculous, but he knew he needed to offer an alternative explanation. One day he happened to read the writings of Francisco Redi. Redi had proved that flies had to reach meat for the maggots to appear, and that if you stopped flies getting to the meat by covering it, no maggots would appear.

Spallanzani was taken with the simplicity of Redi's findings, and he began experiments to show that the tiny living creatures we now call microbes do not arise spontaneously.

He did an experiment much like one Pasteur devised many years later to prove this point. Spallanzani boiled soups of seeds and beans for an hour to kill all microbes, sealed the necks of the flasks by melting the glass, and showed that no new microbes appeared inside the flasks. They could not enter because of the sealed neck.

Microbes Divide and Grow

Spallanzani had read that a Swiss scientist named de Saussure had seen that microbes increased by multiplying—each one split into two, and those two into four, and so on.

Enchanted by this idea, Spallanzani found a way to trap one microbe in a drop of distilled water. Then he watched it through the microscope until he actually saw the microbe grow and divide. The tiny rod-like shape got thinner and thinner in the middle, until it became two small rods held together by no more than a cobweb-thin thread. The process repeated itself. Each rod lengthened, thinned out, and divided into two more rod-like creatures.

Despite the excitement that Spallanzani's work caused in the learned societies of Europe, the novelty of peering into this world of the infinitely small creatures diminished. The old theories that Spallanzani had worked so hard to bury—the theories about the spontaneous generation of living things—began to be the accepted theory once again.

Pasteur's Germ Theory

Then came Louis Pasteur in France. Within thirty years, Pasteur's knowledge had transformed how scientists thought about the world.

An engraving of young Louis Pasteur.

Louis Pasteur proved—and scientists grasped the idea—that the germs of microbes do not arise spontaneously, but travel into matter and liquids from outside agents, such as the dusts of the air. Once Pasteur had convinced scientists of this fact, the way was open to prove the germ theory of disease. This theory states that many diseases are caused by microbes that invade, overwhelm, and weaken a human, animal, or plant body.

The scientists of Pasteur's day realized that if microbes caused diseases, then these microbes needed to be tracked down and caught. Scientists wanted to find ways of controlling, killing, or preventing the microbes from taking hold. Thus, the science of immunology—the knowledge of how to make the body develop its own defenses against the microbes of specific diseases—was born.

To appreciate Pasteur's revolutionary contribution to the world, we need to go back to his beginnings and understand what the world was like when he was born.

Above: *Arbois, on the banks of the Cuisance River, where Louis grew up.*

Right: *Pastel portraits Louis did of his father (right) and mother (below) when he was sixteen.*

Pasteur's Childhood

Louis grew up in France in an area that is not far from Switzerland and the Alps. It is near the Jura Mountains, which form a rugged barrier between Switzerland and France. Here, in the small town of Dole on the river Doubs, Louis was born. He arrived on December 27, 1822, in a house on a street that now bears his name. In 1822, it was called the Rue des Tanneurs, the street of tanners. Louis' father was a tanner. Each house was a tannery where the fresh skins of cattle and sheep were "tanned" and turned into leather.

Louis was just three years old when he and his sisters were loaded into a cart with their furniture and their father's tools, to make the journey to the southeast. There, the family settled in the town of Arbois. There was a tannery at this house, too. There were pits in the yard where the skins could be soaked, a room for his father to sell leather, another for his father's workshop, and space for the family to live above the tannery.

Here, Louis grew up with his three sisters. The town of Arbois was hilly, its squares and arcades shaded by planer trees and poplars. A little river, Cuisance, flowed by the wall of Louis' house. With its nearby fields, the small children of the village could play and fish endlessly. Arbois remained the focus of Louis' young life for many years.

The early life of Louis Pasteur is remarkable for the absence of anything that would have foreshadowed his later life as a great scientist.

In Louis' teens, his talents seemed mainly to be in drawing and painting. At the age of thirteen, he showed his remarkable skill in pastel pictures that he drew of his sisters and mother and of other drawings that show the river that ran by his home in Arbois.

Off to Paris

Young Louis developed one overriding, early ambition—to become a teacher and go to Paris to study at the Ecole Normale Superieure, a school founded by Napoleon Bonaparte to train professors for the schools and colleges of France.

Louis' first attempt at studying in Paris, however, was disastrous. He was sixteen, and his bonds to his family were too strong. He was crippled with homesickness. Louis did not enjoy the excitement of the Latin Quarter with its students thronging the University of the Sorbonne and its cafes humming with young people. Instead, he felt only a longing for his hometown—and the loneliness.

Young Louis' experiment in Paris lasted for only six weeks before his father made the long journey by stagecoach to fetch him home again. Louis returned to the college at Arbois, and went back to his drawing and painting. On his return, he began producing a remarkable set of portraits of friends and acquaintances. Later, Louis went to college in Besançon, only 25 miles (40 kilometers) away from Arbois. There, he seems to have flourished and received much praise for his drawing.

Louis never lost sight of his goal, however. At Besançon, he began to prepare for the Ecole Normale. He was not content with his first results in the entrance exam, for although he got a place there, he came fifteenth out of twenty-two. He decided to leave Besançon, study for another year, and try the test again the following year.

Paris—a Second Time

Louis Pasteur went back to Paris, and this second time was very different from his first miserable experience. To earn money to pay for part of his room and board, Pasteur gave lessons to the younger boys from six until seven in the morning.

Jean Béraud 1889

A painting of Paris by Jean Beraud (1849-1936) that shows how Paris must have looked when Louis arrived there in 1842.

After Pasteur finished tutoring, his day began. Since his classes at his school, College Saint-Louis, didn't start as early as he wished, Pasteur began his day attending lectures at the Sorbonne. He was captivated with "France's first chemist," Jean-Baptiste Dumas, and the energy in his lectures. Of them, Pasteur recalled that Dumas could "set fire to the soul."

During this period, Pasteur's determination to succeed in science seemed to take hold from these lectures by Dumas.

At the end of the school year, Pasteur scored fourth in the exam for the Ecole Normale. In October 1843, shortly before Pasteur's twenty-first birthday, he entered the Ecole Normale to learn how to teach chemistry and physics.

Pasteur's First Explorations

Microbes couldn't have been further from his mind as Pasteur came to the end of his studies at the Ecole Normale and looked around for something special to study—something to give him a chance for independent explorations.

Pasteur knew he wanted to become a first-rate teacher. To reach this goal, he knew he needed to understand everything about the subject so that he would be able to teach the lessons so thoroughly that his young students would be enthusiastic.

Perhaps it was Pasteur's artistic eye that drew him to crystals because they are so delicate and intricate. One of his teachers had shown him a specimen of a salt that had formed crystals. Although the specimen was apparently a very pure salt, it was actually a mixture of three different kinds of crystals. Pasteur was intrigued. Why were there three different kinds of crystals? There must be some reason.

Pasteur's search into the formation of crystals prompted in him the fundamental questions that all scientists face: what are substances made of; and how can we know how matter is built?

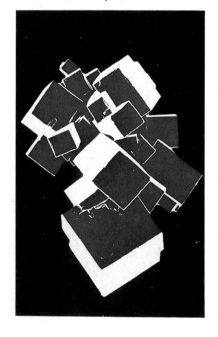

Crystals of pure salt magnified by an electron microscope.

Crystals and Light

Crystals had attracted the attention of scientists for thousands of years. By Pasteur's time, scientists knew what they looked like, but they didn't know a great deal more. Louis' elderly physics teacher, Professor Biot, had also found out that if a beam of light is shone through some crystals, the beam of light doesn't continue in the same straight path. Instead, the beam of light bends.

Pasteur wanted to know why. He was intrigued. This was before scientists understood that the building blocks of substances—what we call atoms—have a specific pattern in each substance.

It was also a time before scientists understood how a group of atoms is arranged to form a molecule, and how an arrangement of molecules makes up a substance—a solid, gas, or liquid. It would be more than half a century before the discovery of radioactivity began to reveal the inner structure of the atom.

The fact that crystals did unexpected things with beams of light made Pasteur wonder if there was a link between the kind of crystal and what it did to light. He wanted to know the connection between the crystal's chemical composition and its combination of ingredients (or what scientists today call its compounds).

Pasteur also wanted to determine the correlation between each crystal's shape and what it did to light. First, Pasteur began by making a careful study of a series of compounds, called tartaric acid and the tartrates. Two forms of tartaric acid crystals were found in the residue that built up inside wine barrels while grape juice fermented.

In his early research, Pasteur noticed that if you made a solution with the first type of crystal in water, it bent a beam of light, as Professor Biot had seen. However, if you made a water solution with the second type of crystal, it did not bend the beam of light! The mystery was that both crystals were identical chemically—that is, they were both made up of exactly the same ingredients.

The First Adventure

Louis Pasteur began to study piles of crystals, looking at them through his magnifying glass. He measured the angles between the different faces in the crystals, dissolving them, forming them again—always struggling to find something that would explain the extraordinary difference in what they did to light. Pasteur could not find the answer to the riddle.

Jean-Baptiste Dumas, Professor of Chemistry at the Sorbonne.

Tartaric acid crystals.

Pasteur's First Discovery About Crystals

As Pasteur peered for the thousandth time through his magnifying glass, it struck him that the crystals, which treated light so differently, were the same in all but one respect. The difference was so subtle that Pasteur hadn't noticed it before! In one form of the crystal, one of the facets sloped one way. In the other, the facets sloped the other way.

With mounting excitement, Pasteur dissolved the different crystals separately in solutions of water. Then he predicted what each would do to a beam of light.

Pasteur's predictions were correct. What was significant about Pasteur's discovery? It showed Pasteur that he could study the structure of a crystal by studying what it did with a beam of light. He also realized that that if he investigated how a crystal behaved, he could tell the structure of how it was built!

The investigation of how substances were built

was still in its infancy. Pasteur's theories opened a new perspective on crystals. His research suggested new methods, new techniques—in fact, a whole new approach to looking at crystals. For the next years, Pasteur was busily engaged in this work. In effect, he was laying the foundations of a new science, the science of stereochemistry, which deals with the arrangement of atoms and groups in molecules.

Pasteur's initial discovery, however, raised all kinds of additional questions. The crystals seemed to be exactly alike, except that they were mirror images of each other. Pasteur wondered about the significance of this one discrepancy. There was a reason for this difference (scientists now call it dissymetry, the absence of symmetry), but Pasteur did not know what the significance was. The meaning behind crystals absorbed Pasteur for the next ten years. Then, an unexpected turn of events propelled him from the world of crystals into the world of another, quite different phenomenon.

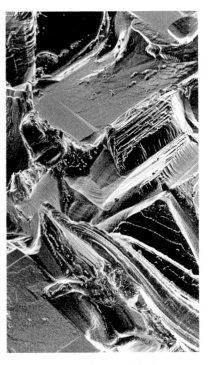

Sea salt crystals magnified 100 times by an electron microscope.

Madame Pasteur

By the end of 1848, Pasteur's time at the Ecole Normale was over. By January of 1849, he had accepted a position as a lecturer in chemistry at the University of Strasbourg. Here, at the age of twenty-six he met and fell in love with Marie Laurent, daughter of the university principal.

Fifteen days later, with the precision of purpose and determination that was so characteristic of Louis Pasteur, he wrote to the principal asking for Marie's hand in marriage. "My family is comfortable, but not rich," he wrote. "All we possess is not worth more than fifty thousand francs, and I have long ago decided to let my sisters have it all. I, therefore, have no fortune whatsoever. All I possess is good health, a willing spirit, and my work.

"I have been a Doctor of Science for eighteen

••••••••••••••••••••••••••

"I woke up every morning with the thought that you wouldn't return my love, and then I wept! My work means nothing to me - to me, who was so devoted to my crystals that when I went to bed I wished the night was not so long, so that I could get back to work quicker!"

Louis, in a letter to Marie Laurent before their marriage

••••••••••••••••••••••••••

months. . . as to the future, all I can say is that, unless my tastes change entirely, I shall devote myself to chemical research."

To Marie's mother, he wrote, "There is nothing in me to attract a young girl's fancy, but my memory tells me that those who have known me very well have loved me very much."

Pasteur seems not to have been at all confident of the answer he would get from Marie. He pleaded with her, "All that I ask, Mademoiselle, is that you will not be hasty in your judgment of me. You might make a mistake. Time will show you that, under a cold and shy outside, which doubtless displeases you, there is a heart full of affection for you."

Marie and Louis were married on May 29, 1849. From the beginning, Marie seems to have accepted Louis' overwhelming absorption in his work, and to have grown used to a husband whose mind was preoccupied with the events of his laboratory. She devoted her life to supporting him, freeing him from household cares, helping him and loving him, and allowing him complete freedom for his research.

Marie was much more than a homemaker for her husband. Emile Roux, one of Pasteur's pupils who later became famous for his own work on vaccines, documented how Madame Pasteur discussed Pasteur's work with him, spurred his thinking on, and was one of Pasteur's best scientific collaborators.

For the next five years, the couple lived in Strasbourg. Louis was absorbed with his crystals and his teaching. While in Strasbourg three of their five children were born: daughter Jeanne, followed a year later by a son, Jean-Baptiste, and two years later, by baby Cecile.

Professor Pasteur

In September of 1854, Pasteur had a new challenge. He was made Professor of Chemistry and

Dean of the Faculty of Science at Lille. Lille was a prosperous industrial city in the north of France where a great many gentlemen were in the trade of fermenting beetroot juice to make alcohol.

Pasteur was just thirty-two and very young for a position of such responsibility. It was an outstanding achievement. He took his teaching seriously, and he wanted to infuse his students with a similar sense of awe in nature that he felt. "Has anybody a son," he asked a gathering of prosperous manufacturers and their wives, "who would not be interested if you gave him a potato and told him 'from that potato you can make sugar, from sugar you can make alcohol, from alcohol vinegar?'"

The students of Lille were interested. Louis Pasteur's lectures were events not to be missed. He even took his pupils on tours of the factories and foundries that made steel and metalworks of France and Belgium.

The Puzzling Process of Fermentation

One day in 1856, Monsieur Bigo came to Pasteur to ask for his advice. (Pasteur was his son's teacher.) Monsieur Bigo manufactured alcohol from beet sugar, but he had a problem. Most of the time, the process of changing beet sugar into alcohol in his factory went well. In some of the vats, however, the juice was going sour. The spoiled vats were costing Monsieur Bigo thousands of francs a day in lost income.

Pasteur knew nothing about the manufacturing and fermentation of alcohol. He had some thoughts on fermentation, however, because his research studies had revolved around crystals found in wine barrels that had formed during the process of fermentation. No one knew much about how the fermentation occurred—just that it happened.

There would have been no need for any investigation at all if proper fermentation occurred every time.

This painting by Edouard Debat-Ponsan shows workers in a French vineyard.

The spoiled vats were a puzzle, and Monsieur Bigo hoped that a man of science like Pasteur might offer some new suggestions. At Bigo's request, Pasteur went along to the factory to have a look. He sniffed at the vats of fermenting sugar-beet juice. These were the vats where the juice was turning to alcohol.

In another group of vats, it was a very different matter. All Pasteur could see was a slimy, sour mess! He studied the sour liquid, but could offer no explanations. He decided he needed to take a closer look in his laboratory. So he put some of the sour liquid into bottles and took it to his laboratory.

Fermentation Under the Microscope

Pasteur placed a drop of liquid from a good vat under his microscope. What was he looking for? He didn't really know. Perhaps there would be some familiar crystals that would help Pasteur understand the fermentation process.

With the magnifying power of the microscope, Pasteur saw that the tiny drop of liquid from the good vat was filled with minute globules—little yellowish round and oval shapes that swarmed with darker specks. They were far smaller than any crystal he had ever seen! Pasteur searched his memory for some clue as to what they were. After much thought, Pasteur realized these must be the yeast cells that scientists knew were always in the mixture when sugar-beet juice or grapes were fermenting. Scientists had known they were there, but they did not agree what they were doing there.

The Yeast Was Alive!

The more Pasteur watched, the more he became convinced—with mounting excitement—that the yeast globules were alive. He believed that the yeasts were somehow at the bottom of this fermentation process—and that they were causing fermentation!

"Chance in one guise or another, has frequently attended the birth of discovery. Chance evidence comes to everybody, but only a genius is capable of interpreting it correctly. Genius is not enough. Without adequate scientific training, even the most intelligent individual remains incapable of interpreting the play of accidental factors, and incapable of experimentally reproducing some phenomena which chance has thrown in his way, so as to ascertain whether his deductions are valid or not."

Hilaire Cuny, from "Louis Pasteur, his theories."

Pasteur also recalled faintly that other scientists in Germany had thought the yeasts were alive. In fact, a scientist named Cagniard-Latour in France had poked around beer breweries and had reported that he had seen little buds on the yeasts.

Pasteur peered through his microscope again. Yes! He could see the buds. Hour after hour, he watched, utterly absorbed in this miniature world. First one—and then another—bud grew larger. When they split apart, there were two yeast globules where there had been only one. Pasteur had seen the yeast grow and multiply. The buds were feeding on the beet juice and giving off alcohol and carbon dioxide!

Still, this didn't solve Pasteur's problem—or, ultimately, Monsieur Bigo's problem. Why were some of the vats sour and not others? Pasteur went back to peering into the microscope. He placed a drop of the slimy liquid under the microscope. There were no round globules of yeast. Pasteur picked up the

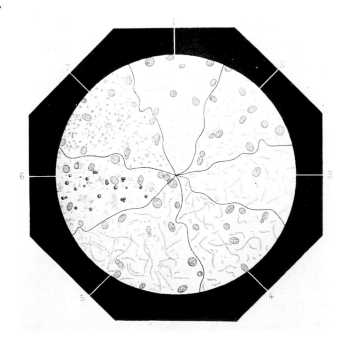

This is a sketch by Louis Pasteur from Studies on Beer, published in 1876. It shows the microorganisms that cause fermentation in various liquids.

28

bottle and looked at it. There were specks stuck to the inside and floating in the liquid.

The Black Rods

Pasteur needed to know if there were any specks in the healthy liquid. He looked, but could find none. With some difficulty, Pasteur managed to get one of the specks from the slimy liquid into a drop of pure water and under his microscope. He stared in disbelief. Millions of tiny black rods were busy in some kind of weird, shimmering dance. Pasteur tried to work out how big each rod was. He determined that each one couldn't be more than one twenty-five thousandth of an inch long!

Like Leeuwenhoek and Spallanzani, Pasteur fell under the spell of these creatures. Pasteur realized what was happening. The rod-shaped creatures had overrun the yeast cells and had stopped them from making alcohol. Instead, the tiny rod-like organisms were manufacturing lactic acid—the same ingredient that makes milk sour.

Pasteur relied on his instincts as a scientist. He didn't jump to conclusions. Instead, he knew he had to be certain about what was happening. Pasteur returned to the beet factory. He studied more samples, and each time in the vats that had turned sour, he found the rods. When the rods were present, there was no alcohol. Instead, there was only the acid of sour milk.

The Alcohol Industry Is Saved

Pasteur couldn't say how the rods got into the vats, but he suspected that it was something transmitted by the air. He told Monsieur Bigo how to get good alcohol: test the liquid from every vat under a microscope. If only yeast cells could be seen, all would be well. If even one of the rod-like creatures had made an appearance, Monsieur Bigo would

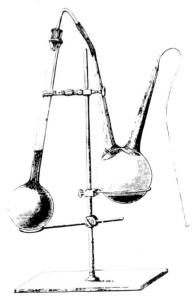

An engraving of an apparatus Pasteur used in his experiments on beer. The flask on the left contained the wort (ingredients that became beer after fermentation). The flask on the right contained a pure yeast culture.

The equipment developed by Pasteur to pasteurize beer.

need to throw the entire vat away—and destroy every bit of it.

To the alcohol manufacturers of Lille, Louis Pasteur was a hero. Their industry had been saved from ruin.

The scientist was fascinated by his experience in Bigo's sugar-beet factory—he couldn't put the rod-like creatures out of his mind. Pasteur was certain that the rods caused the sour milk acid and that the yeasts caused the alcohol. A picture took hold in Pasteur's mind: rods and yeasts doing battle with each other. It was a picture that motivated him in his work on the microbes of disease.

Microbes

Pasteur couldn't study the rods properly because they were all tangled up in the sugar-beet pulp. He needed to find a place for the rods to grow, something in which he could see them clearly.

First, Pasteur tried sugar mixed with water because he knew there was always sugar in fermenting liquid. When he examined the mixture under the microscope, there was nothing. Next Pasteur turned himself into a scientific cook, trying all sorts of mixtures. Every time, he found with disappointment, that the rods did not grow.

Pasteur asked himself a question: what about making a "yeast" soup? Pasteur put dried yeast into water and added a carefully measured amount of sugar. Then he boiled the soup so it would be completely free of any microbes. After he had finished boiling it, he strained the soup until it was perfectly clear.

Pasteur added a further step: would the rods from the sick fermentations in Bigo's factory grow in this germ-free yeast soup? He put a speck from a sick fermentation into a flask of the soup. Then he carried the flask to his incubating oven where the mixture could be kept warm.

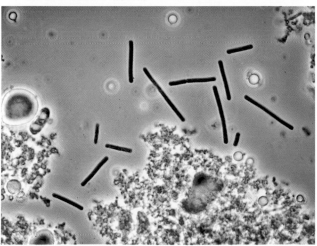

Above: *Modern stainless steel wine vats.*

Left: *Pasteur's "dancing black rods," were the bacillus he detected in spoiled sugar-beet vats. Here they are shown in yogurt.*

Whenever Pasteur looked into the incubator at the flask, he could see that nothing was happening. He began to feel discouraged, but he was certain— in fact, very certain— that his hunch regarding the rods was correct.

When the waiting had stretched to two days, Pasteur saw something—bubbles, and little puffs of gas, curling up through the soup. He squinted in the half-light, hardly daring to hope. They were coming from the speck he had sown! Surely these specks hadn't been in the soup yesterday!

Black Rods—By the Millions

Pasteur placed a drop of the liquid under the microscope, and stared at it in delight! There were millions of rods! The speck had spawned others. The acid that had appeared in his yeast soup was the same as the acid of sour milk.

Still, Pasteur proceeded cautiously. He took some rods from the contaminated yeast soup and put them into a freshly boiled, germ-free yeast soup. Then he waited again. The same thing happened. Each rod grew and eventually split into two rods.

Next, Pasteur experimented by putting some rods in fresh milk. The milk soured, and the rods multiplied. Pasteur repeated the experiment again and again, until he was absolutely certain about the connection between adding rods to a germ-free environment that then became acidic. Each time he added a tiny drop of rods to a clear soup, millions of new rods always appeared, and they always made the acid of sour milk.

The Mystery Solved

Pasteur had solved the mystery of fermentation, one that had remained unexplained for ten thousand years! The little globules of yeast were the cause of a fermentation process that changed sugar

"To believe one has discovered an important scientific fact, to long to announce it, and yet to restrain oneself for days, weeks, sometimes even years; to strive to disprove one's own experiments; to publish one's discovery only after exhausting every alternative possibility— yes, the task is a hard one. But when. . . certainty is reached, the reward is one of the keenest joys of which the human soul is capable."

Louis Pasteur

into alcohol. The rods were the cause of the bad fermentation that produced a sour result.

In August of 1857, Pasteur presented his finding in a paper that he read to the Lille Scientific Society. In his presentation, he explained that fermentation was a living process, caused by microscopic living creatures that were, in effect, performing a "giant's" work. Those who listened—many of them Pasteur's students—were enthralled. Pasteur wrote to his old teacher, Dumas, about his findings. He also prepared a statement for the Academy of Science in Paris, where reports on science throughout the world were read and discussed.

Pasteur's findings negated the accepted theories of several of the most respected scientists. These scientists believed that fermentation was no more than a chemical reaction between substances. Present-day scientists now know they were partly right: a substance produced by the yeast causes alcoholic fermentation through a chemical reaction.

Pasteur, however, was right when he insisted that without yeast—a living organism—no alcoholic fermentation could take place! Pasteur's work on fermentation showed that microbes cause fermentation in many different substances. Pasteur also developed ways of preventing wine, vinegar, and beer from spoiling—by killing harmful microbes with heat. This process, called pasteurization, is named after him. Today, every glass of germ-free pasteurized milk is a testimony to Louis Pasteur.

Pioneer of the Germ Theory

Pasteur's studies on fermentation convinced him that microbes were at the root of many useful tasks in the world—and at the heart of dangerous things, too.

At the end of 1857, a new era began in Pasteur's life. He was called back to his old school, the Ecole Normale in Paris, to become Administrator and

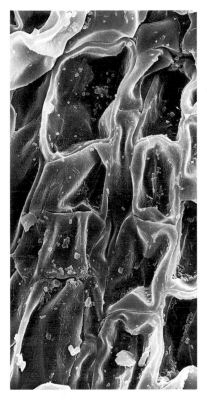

Wine yeast on the surface of a wine bottle cork.

• •

"Nothing is more agreeable to a man who has made science his career than to increase the number of discoveries, but his cup of joy is full when the result of his observations is put to immediate practical use."

Louis Pasteur

• •

Director of Scientific Studies. It was at this point that Pasteur confronted an old idea: the theory of spontaneous generation.

Scientists who were Pasteur's contemporaries knew that humans, animals, or insects, were produced only by parents of their own kind. But many believed that among microorganisms, spontaneous generation happened.

Everything in Pasteur's fermentation work led him to believe that microbes were already in the air, but that people only noticed them when they landed on solid matter or when they were in liquids. Still, they were only visible with a microscope.

Pasteur was only happy with things he could prove. As an old man, he was to say, "If I had to live

Fashionable Paris. Louis once wrote to his father, "Here, more than anywhere, we see vice and virtue, honesty and dishonesty, riches and poverty, perpetually colliding and interweaving."

Left: *Pasteur's two attic rooms, his first "laboratory" at the Ecole Normale.*

my life over again, I would try always to remember that admirable precept of Bossuet: 'The greatest disorder of the mind is to believe that things are so because we wish them to be so.'"

Pasteur knew that the only sure way to convince skeptics was to offer solid proof. He realized that fermentation and putrefaction—or rotting—never took place unless microbes were present. But it was generally believed that the microbes in corpses and rotten meat, for example, were caused by the rotting. Pasteur, however, believed the microbes themselves caused the rotting. Everything in his research pointed to that conclusion. But how could he prove it?

The Search for Proof

Pasteur knew he needed to find a way to show that microbes get into things from the outside. He knew he needed to kill all the microbes in a sealed container, and then show that no new ones had appeared. Pasteur set about devising an experiment, much like Spallanzani's a century before. Pasteur filled glass flasks with a sugary yeast soup and boiled each flask to kill any microbes in it. While the liquid boiled, he sealed it inside by melting the glass at the tip of the neck.

Pasteur divided the sealed flasks into two groups. He snapped off the tip of the necks of one group with pincers to allow air to enter. Then he sealed them shut again by melting the glass. He kept all the flasks in the second group sealed. Then he put both groups in his incubating oven to keep them warm enough for any microbes to grow.

The results were unmistakable. In the flasks that Pasteur had opened and then resealed, yeasts and other fungi had grown. In the flasks he had left sealed, nothing had grown.

In the end, Pasteur proved that germs came only from the outside. The spontaneous generation supporters retaliated. Cutting off the air, they said, stopped spontaneous generation; microbes needed natural, unheated air to burst into spontaneous life!

The Final Proof

While his opponents debated the subject, Pasteur devised an experiment to prove the microbes were airborne. He was convinced that it was not the air itself, but the dusts in the air that carried the microbes. However, as much as he tried, he could not find a way to let air into his flasks without also letting microbes in.

Pasteur was rescued by Professor Balard, an elderly chemistry professor who liked to wander around the laboratories looking at others' work. One day he strolled into Pasteur's laboratory and found Pasteur wrestling with his predicament. Like Biot, Dumas, and others, Professor Balard agreed with Pasteur about germs and air. Balard put his chemist's brain to the problem of Pasteur's flasks and his need for dust-free air. At last, he came up with the solution: prepare the flasks, then heat and bend the necks in a long downward S-shape. Air would be able to pass along the S-shape, but dust would fall downwards with the force of gravity and would not be able to travel around the bends.

With great excitement, Pasteur set up Balard's experiment. This time, as the liquid cooled, the air was drawn in, but the dust and the microbes stuck in the long, curving neck. The flasks remained clear, without contamination. When Pasteur shook some of the liquid and flooded the swan-shaped necks with the clear liquid, the liquid picked up the dust and then returned to the belly of the flask. This liquid then became filled with multiplying microbes!

Even today, over a century later, Pasteur's swan-necked flasks are still clear, proving the simple

"There is here no question of religion, philosophy, atheism, materialism, or spiritualism. I might even add they do not matter to me as a scientist. It is a question of fact; when I took it up, I was as ready to be convinced by experiments that spontaneous generation exists as I am now persuaded that those who believe it are blindfolded."

Louis Pasteur

The original swan-necked flasks used by Pasteur in his experiments on germs in the air.

truth of Pasteur's experiment and the simple generosity of scientists like Professor Balard, who only wanted the truth to emerge.

The Search for Pure Air—Again

Pasteur reasoned that the amount of dust in the air would vary in different places. He predicted that there would be more microbes in a busy street in Paris than at the top of a mountain. What he needed to do was to show that there were different amounts of microbes in the air depending on the place.

Pasteur and his assistants prepared the sealed flasks of yeast soup. Then, they carried ten to the cellars of the Paris Observatory. Another ten were taken to the yard of the observatory. Twenty were taken to a hillside near Pasteur's hometown of Arbois, and the last twenty were carried by mule to the top of Mount Blanc.

Of the ten flasks opened in the cellars, where the air was still and Pasteur had predicted there would

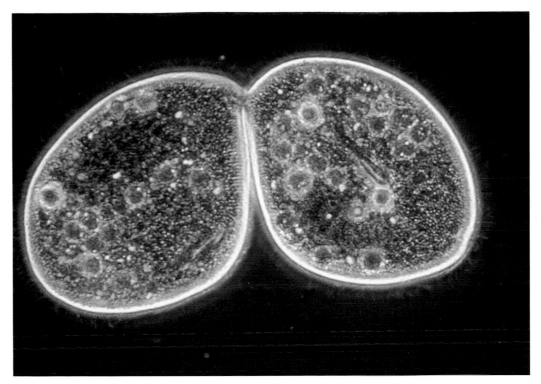

be little dust, only one developed microbes. In the dirty yard of the observatory, ten out of ten went bad. On the hillside near Arbois, only eight out of twenty grew microbes. And out of the twenty flasks taken up Mont Blanc, only one developed microbes.

In November 1860, Pasteur presented his results to the Academy of Science. To those present he said of the flasks, "They enable us, in my opinion, to state definitely that the dusts suspended in the atmosphere are the exclusive origin, the initial, indispensable condition for the existence of life in the liquids."

Pasteur added, with his unfailing sense of vision, "What would be most desirable of all would be to carry these studies far enough to prepare the way for serious research into the origin of different diseases."

Pasteur observed that many microbes increase by dividing. This photograph shows protozoa in the final stages of division into two microorganisms.

Years of Dedication

Over the next ten years, Louis Pasteur answered all of the objections of his opponents through his meticulous research. Some of the opposition was based on scientific grounds. Other opposition came from established scientists who were jealous of such a confident young man—one who always seemed to be right.

Despite his critics, Pasteur conducted his experiments in public for the Academy of Science. The positive results exonerated him from criticism.

In 1862, when Pasteur was nearly forty, he was elected to the Academy. At the Academy, his lectures both inspired and informed his fellow scientists. Many of them were eager to grasp the new understandings of science that Pasteur carefully explained.

The decades of the 1850s and 1860s were exciting ones for science—and for the world. In Pasteur's private life, however, they were also years of tragedy. In September of 1859, his eldest daughter Jeanne died suddenly of typhoid fever. She was only nine years old. We are not told much about the events surrounding this tragedy, but many people feel the tragedy gave Pasteur a new zeal that may not have happened except from this loss. Some theorize that Pasteur's new determination was key to finding new ways to control disease.

Germs, Germs—Everywhere!

Pasteur decided that the world at large must learn about germs! In April of 1864, he spoke at the Sorbonne to a large audience of scientists, students, ministers of state, famous authors, and even a princess. He plunged the hall into darkness. Then Pasteur shone a beam of light across the room to show millions of dust particles suspended in the air. He spoke to his spellbound listeners about the drifting multitudes of germs within.

Then Pasteur showed his two flasks, one with its yeast soup clouded with microbes and the other

Top: *Louis Pasteur and his wife in 1889.*

Bottom: *Pasteur with his granddaughter.*

with its yeast soup still clear. It had been four years since he had first performed the experiment, and the soup was still protected from the germs in the dust by the long, curving neck of the flask.

"What is the difference between the two?" Pasteur asked his fascinated audience. "They are full of the same liquid, they are full of the same air, and they are both open. The only difference is this: in this flask, the dust of the air and its germs can fall into it and reach the liquid and produce microscopic beings. In this other, it is impossible—or very difficult—for the germs of the air to reach the liquid."

At about the same time, the winemakers in his hometown of Arbois were having problems. Some of their wine was going sour, like vinegar, and would not keep for any length of time. Pasteur

This engraving from the French science magazine la Nature *in 1884 shows Louis Pasteur at work in his laboratory at the École Normale.*

Pasteur experimented with heating wine until the harmful microbes were killed.

Opposite: *An operating room in the middle of the nineteenth century.*

turned his microscope on the wine, and discovered the culprits—the microbes lurking in the vats that made the wine sour and bitter. He experimented until he could tell the winemakers exactly how much to heat the wine after it had finished fermenting. Pasteur told the winemakers that this process would kill the bad microbes without damaging the wine itself. Pasteur had invented pasteurization.

Lister's Application of the Germ Theory

In Scotland, a doctor named Joseph Lister, Professor of Surgery in Edinburgh, read of Pasteur's proof of germs in the air. Lister had been searching for a way to control infection in hospitals. Experimenting swiftly with ways of killing germs, Lister brought about a transformation in hospital cleanliness and sterilization procedures.

In Pasteur's time, hospitals were grim places. More often than not, people died not from the illnesses they had come in with, but from infections they developed once they were in the hospital. The death rate after operations was very high. Many of

Joseph Lister, was the first to apply Louis Pasteur's germ theory to control disease in hospitals.

Lister's patients seemed to be getting better, but around the fourth day, they would develop an infection in their wounds and die not long after.

By 1867 in Lister's wards, all the instruments and equipment used to dress wounds were dipped in a strong solution of carbolic acid to destroy germs. Medical workers also scrubbed their hands with carbolic acid, and carbolic acid was sprayed on the wounds during the operation. Later the wound was washed with carbolic solution, and Lister used antiseptic materials for dressings. Another advance came later, in France, after the Franco-Prussian war of 1871, when surgeons began to disinfect instruments and filter the air around wounds.

Before these precautions were taken, at least fifty out of every hundred patients had died after operations. Even in the early trials of his new methods, Lister reduced the death rate to fifteen out of every hundred, and then to three out of every hundred.

Years later, in 1874, Lister wrote a letter to Louis Pasteur. "Allow me," Lister said, "to take this opportunity to tender you my most cordial thanks for. . . furnishing me with the principles upon which alone the antiseptic system can be carried out."

The Germ Theory of Disease—Again

The question of what actually caused disease in the body was still open. Most doctors believed that disease was "in us and of us and brought into being by us." But the idea that disease and the process of rotting were connected was also an old one. Two hundred years before Pasteur, the English scientist Robert Boyle had said, "He that thoroughly understands the nature of ferments and fermentations, shall probably be much better able than he that ignores them, to give a fair account of diverse phenomena of several diseases."

In the end, Pasteur was pushed by an unexpected combination of circumstances to take his first steps toward discovering what caused diseases in the body.

The Silkworm Doctor

In 1865, Professor Dumas, Pasteur's old friend and now a member of the French Senate, had an urgent favor to ask. At the request of France's government, Dumas wanted Pasteur to investigate an epidemic that was killing silkworms. The epidemic was devastating the French silk industry.

Pasteur was reluctant to go to France. He had no knowledge of silkworms, but, Dumas was an old friend. Pasteur; Duclaux, one of his best pupils; and three other students from the Ecole Normale went to Alais—Dumas' own village. In a rented cottage, they set up a laboratory to attempt to solve the puzzle behind the silkworm epidemic.

Weaving silk in a London cottage.

Pasteur set up his microscope and examined hundreds of silk chrysalises and moths. Within a few days, he decided that a little globule seen in diseased worms, moths, and chrysalides (the pupa form of a moth when it is enclosed in a cocoon) was a sign of the disease. He concluded that the silkworm disease started with mature moths that produced diseased eggs. These eggs developed into diseased worms, chrysalides, and moths. Pasteur decided he had solved part of the mystery.

What immediate advice did Pasteur have for the silkworm breeders? Check each moth after she had laid her eggs for any globules in her body. If there were any globules, then the eggs would be diseased and must be destroyed. If the moth's body was clear of globules, the eggs would be sound, and healthy worms would emerge.

Disaster!

Pasteur had to wait until the eggs hatched in the spring to find out if his predictions were right. In the spring, Pasteur learned a bitter lesson. When the eggs hatched, they produced diseased worms.

Pasteur went back to his microscope to find out where he had made a mistake. He tried new experiments with puzzling results. There were dying worms that didn't have globules, and live worms that did.

Pasteur's pupils were not discouraged. They went on with the experiments he asked them to do. The work continued, month after month.

It was an epic of scientific investigation and struggle. In the end, Pasteur and his team found where the mistake had been. There were two diseases—not one. One involved globules, and another disease involved microscopic creatures. They determined that the globule was alive. It was a microbe. It multiplied, spreading throughout the moth, egg, or worm.

By 1865, a silkworm disease had already devastated the silk industries of Italy, Spain, Austria, and even China, where the silk industry had thrived for more than 2,000 years.

Above: *A silk moth on silk cocoons.*

Left: *Silkworms consume the leaves of the mulberry tree.*

Left bottom: *A silk mother emerging from the chrysalis.*

Opposite:
French newspaper, Le Petit Journal, *showing the "Grim Reaper" and people dying and dead from cholera.*

Through his research and recommendations, Pasteur saved the silkworm and the silk industry. He also learned how vital it was to be unfailingly methodical and complete in his experiments. Pasteur had found out that healthy worms became sick when the droppings from sick worms soiled the mulberry leaves they ate. The second disease that had confused him, flacherie, was passed on through the worms' intestines. In effect, Pasteur showed the importance of the environment in spreading disease.

Personal Tragedy

A cholera epidemic had broken out in Paris and Marseilles, and 200 people were dying every day. Pasteur knew the personal impact of disease. He had already lost his eldest daughter, Jeanne, to typhoid fever. In September 1865, his two-year-old daughter, Camille, became ill and died. Only a few months later, twelve-year-old Cecile also fell victim to typhoid fever. By May 1866, she too was dead.

The personal losses of his children took a toll on Pasteur. He found himself in the frustrating position of watching doctors who could not save his children. In October 1868, Pasteur was back in Paris. On October 19, he woke up with a strange, tingling sensation on his left side.

By afternoon, Pasteur was convulsing and shivering. Still, he had promised to read a note to the Academy of Science that evening on behalf of an Italian scientist. When he came home, Pasteur went to bed, still feeling ill. During the night, his condition worsened. He could no longer speak or move. The whole left side of his body was paralyzed. He was nearly forty-six, and he had had a stroke. The doctors thought he was going to die.

Le Petit Journal

ADMINISTRATION
61, RUE LAFAYETTE, 61
Les manuscrits ne sont pas rendus

5 CENT.

SUPPLÉMENT ILLUSTRÉ

5 CENT.

ABONNEMENTS

27me Année

Numéro 1.150

On s'abonne sans frais
dans tous les bureaux de poste

DIMANCHE 1er DÉCEMBRE 1912

	AUX MOIS	UN AN
SEINE et SEINE-ET-OISE..	2 fr.	3 fr. 50
DÉPARTEMENTS........	2 fr.	4 fr. »
ÉTRANGER........	2 50	5 fr. »

LE CHOLÉRA

A Slow Recovery

As usual, Louis Pasteur defied predictions. He managed to speak again, at first only in single words. A week later, he was dictating notes to his assistants, but he was paralyzed in his left arm and leg. He refused to let it stop him from working. Within three months, Pasteur was off to Alais to see how the silkworm work was progressing.

Pasteur could no longer handle the scientific apparatus himself so he became dependent on his assistants to perform the careful experiments he devised. The more he studied silkworms, the more certain Pasteur became of a link between the fermentation of yeasts and the diseases that affected animals and humans. To fellow scientists, he proclaimed, "It is in the power of man to make parasitic illnesses disappear from the face of the globe, if the doctrine of spontaneous generation is wrong, as I am sure it is."

Doctors as a group dismissed these predictions. It was a country doctor in Germany who turned these predictions into fact and realized the significance of what Louis Pasteur had shown.

One Microbe, One Disease

In the heart of the farm country in East Prussia, a doctor named Robert Koch was frustrated by his inability to do anything to cure disease. He was given a microscope for his birthday by his wife, who hoped it would help to quiet his restlessness. One day, Koch turned his microscope on the gluey black blood from animals that had died of anthrax. It was a disease that was wiping out herds of sheep and cattle throughout Europe. At once, Koch saw the rod-like microbes swarming in the sick blood.

Following his curiosity, Koch proved that the rod-like things were alive. Then he proved they multiplied. He discovered they were never found in healthy animals, and that they could survive

Louis Pasteur, with members of his research team.

"He had to fight ignorance, prejudice, the innate conservatism of his eminent colleagues and of the medical establishment. He fought this fight, with kindness, good humor, and a basic equanimity, which yet allowed the passion of his 'exalted mind' to drive him on and to inspire other... men with some of his own enthusiasm."

H.I. Winner, from "Louis Pasteur and Microbiology"

shriveled into spores, lurking until they could burst into activity again. Koch determined that the anthrax microbe (bacillus anthracis)—and this alone—caused the disease of anthrax.

In April 1876, three years after he had started work on the problem, Koch told his former professors that he had proved that one microbe caused one disease. He pointed to his research on anthrax.

A new search began to find the microbes that had been killing people year after year—diseases such as cholera, typhoid, tuberculosis, pneumonia, syphilis, diphtheria, and the Russian plague. In the following decades, scientists worked to track down the microbes, grow them, and learn how they lived and died.

The Beginnings of Immunology

With increasing clarity during these years, Pasteur saw disease as a form of struggle for existence, a kind of contest between the microbes and the tissues they were trying to invade.

During his travels around France, Pasteur had seen a cow that had anthrax but had recovered naturally from it. He had seen that the cow did not die when injected with powerful anthrax bacilli. The idea took root in Pasteur's mind that having the disease somehow caused the body to develop a resistance against it.

Louis Pasteur was not a doctor, and there were many doctors who thought that laboratory scientists like Pasteur should not meddle in medicine. However, there were enough doctors who recognized the impact that Pasteur's research was having. In 1873, Louis Pasteur was elected to the Academy of Medicine.

At about the same time, Pasteur took on some young doctors as his assistants—Dr. Joubert, Dr. Roux, and Dr. Chamberland. They brought the

Robert Koch was the first to prove that a specific microbe causes a specific disease.

techniques of medical practice as more and more of Pasteur's work turned to the search for some way to control disease-causing microbes.

Chance—and a Great Breakthrough

In 1878, Pasteur began to study the microbe that caused a poultry disease known as chicken cholera. It had recently killed a tenth of the chickens in France. Pasteur was growing the microbes in chicken broth, and had seen that when injected into chickens, it killed the chickens within days.

It was summertime when the research project began, and Pasteur and his assistants went on vacation. The culture of chicken cholera microbes was put on a shelf and forgotten. On his return from vacation, Pasteur was about to throw away the culture of chicken cholera microbes when he changed his mind.

Pasteur injected the culture into a hen. The hen became mildly sick, but recovered quickly. In the days that followed, the hen stayed well, happily strutting around its cage.

Pasteur injected more hens with the old culture. They joined the first hen in strutting around the cages. Next, Pasteur injected the hens with a fresh culture, but this culture he determined was strong enough to kill. Each hen got the killer dose.

They were unaffected. Then Pasteur injected the fresh culture into another batch of hens, ones that had not been inoculated with the old culture. They all died.

"In the field of experimentation chance favors the prepared mind," Pasteur once said. He understood immediately what the successful inoculations meant.

Edward Jenner, an English doctor, had used the microbes of the mild disease of cowpox to vaccinate against smallpox, and this was now widely used in Europe. The methods were based on using a disease known not to be harmful to people.

Opposite, top: *Bacillus anthracis, the microbe that causes anthrax.*

Opposite, bottom: *Bacillus anthracis shown in animal tissue. In humans, it attacks the lungs and causes skin ulcers.*

Could Pasteur successfully repeat the results of the vaccine? Pasteur decided to call the treatment vaccination after Jenner's methods. This term vaccination is still used to name the technique of preventing a disease by inoculating in advance against it, by immunization.

Pasteur wondered how many other microbes could be grown in a laboratory, weakened, and used as vaccines? For the rest of his life, Pasteur searched for ways to weaken the ability of microbes enough to force the body's natural defenses to arm themselves against the disease.

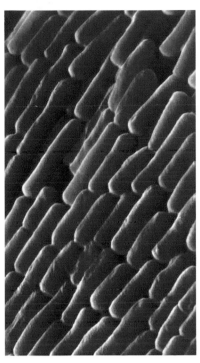

The Anthrax Vaccine

For some time, Pasteur had also been studying the disease of anthrax, just as Robert Koch had also done. The cattle-rearing provinces of France were losing thousands of cattle each year. Flocks of sheep were also devastated—sometimes as many as half of them died from anthrax. People also died from anthrax—a tiny scratch had the power to kill.

The search for an anthrax vaccine took many years. Pasteur and his team started work on discovering the mysteries of the disease in 1877. In 1879, they made the chicken cholera discovery. Not until February of 1881, did Pasteur believe that he and his team had succeeded in developing an anthrax vaccine.

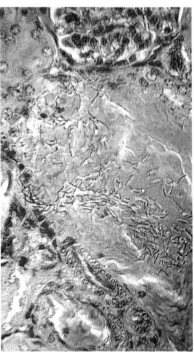

The Great Challenge

Pasteur accepted a challenge from the farmers in Melun, near Paris to test the anthrax vaccine in public. In May of 1881, at the farm of Pouilly-le-Fort, ministers of state, animal doctors, farmers, scientists, and reporters gathered to see Pasteur and his assistants—Roux, Chamberland, and Thuillier—vaccinate the sheep.

Twenty-five sheep received two vaccinations. The first used weakened microbes—ones that were

A drawing from a French magazine of 1882 showing a doctor vaccinating sheep according to Louis Pasteur's method.

old and weak. Twelve days later, the same twenty-five sheep were vaccinated with fresher, stronger microbes in order to build up their resistance. Another twenty-five sheep received no vaccinations at all. The two groups were kept in separate grazing areas. Then all fifty sheep were given fatal doses of powerful anthrax microbes.

Louis was confident in public, but privately he was nervous, unable to sleep, unable to open the telegram when it arrived from Pouilly-le-Fort with the results of the experiment. Madame Pasteur opened the letter for him. The results showed that all the sheep that had received the vaccinations were still healthy. All the unvaccinated sheep were dead or dying. The vaccine had worked!

Pasteur's laboratories rushed to make the vaccine. Roux, Chamberland, and Thuillier traveled around France injecting animals with the miracle drug. In under a year, hundreds of thousands of animals had been vaccinated. The following year,

500,000 sheep in France and 80,000 oxen had received the vaccine.

There were, however, some problems with the vaccine. It was difficult to make the drug pure enough, and sometimes the vaccine actually caused anthrax. Other times, the vaccine was so weak, it didn't work at all. But a giant leap in medical knowledge had taken place—a viable vaccine had been prepared that could prevent a disease before it caused devastation to humans or animals.

Pasteur's Final Crusade

Many people remember Pasteur not for the anthrax vaccine but because he discovered an effective treatment for rabies. In Pasteur's time, rabies in humans meant almost certain death. Humans get rabies when bitten by a rabid dog or animal.

Pasteur and his team reasoned that the microbe that caused rabies was probably in the central nervous system. Pasteur and his assistants took nerve tissue—fragments from the spinal cord of a mad dog that had died from rabies—and injected it into a rabbit. Two weeks later, the rabbit had rabies. When it died, they took some of its spinal cord and injected it into another rabbit. They did this until the rabies had been transferred twenty-five times.

By March of 1885 Pasteur wrote to a friend, "I have demonstrated this year that one can vaccinate dogs or render them immune to rabies. I have not dared to treat humans bitten by rabid dogs."

The Boy with Rabies

One Monday morning—July 6, 1885—nine-year-old Joseph Meister arrived at Pasteur's laboratory with his mother. He had been bitten on the face, hands, and body by a mad dog in his village in Alsace two days before.

What was Pasteur to do? The vaccine wasn't

Pasteur's search for a rabies cure took more than three years.

"If the animal screamed at all, Pasteur was immediately filled with compassion, and tried to comfort and encourage the victim, in a way that would have seemed ludicrous if it had not been touching."

Dr. Emile Roux

The shepherd boy, Jupille, being inoculated against rabies.

ready for human tests. He asked colleagues from the Academy of Medicine if the boy would develop rabies. They counted the boy's wounds, and said he would. Yet, without sufficient testing having been completed, Pasteur's vaccine might kill the boy. If Pasteur did not inoculate him, there was a good chance Joseph would die anyway, or become completely paralyzed.

Pasteur decided to vaccinate Joseph Meister. On the evening of July 6, Pasteur supervised a doctor who injected the extract from the weakened spinal cord of a rabbit that had died of rabies fifteen days before. Each day, the boy was given a vaccine with a stronger extract. Joseph's bites healed, and he never contracted rabies.

We will never know how many people survived because of Pasteur's vaccine, but it is certain that most would have died. The crucial jump in treatment had been made—from animals to humans.

Above: *Louis Pasteur's rooms at the Pasteur Institute in Paris, where he spent most of his last years.*

Left: *A statue of Joseph Meister and the rabid dog that attacked him stands on the grounds of the Pasteur Institute in Paris.*

Dr. Emile Roux, one of Pasteur's assistants, injecting a horse during his investigation of diphtheria.

Ellie Metchnikov, one of Pasteur's pupils, unraveled ways in which the body fights back against microbes and develops immunities.

The Academy of Science decided to found an institute to be called the Pasteur Institute, to organize the treatment of rabies.

The world responded, and money poured in.

Pasteur's Final Years

Pasteur continued working until he was nearly seventy. In 1887, when he was sixty-four, he had another stroke. In November 1888, the Pasteur Institute officially opened, and Pasteur was able to see his pupils and collaborators continue in the spirit of enthusiasm and determination that had been the guiding inspiration of his own life.

Pasteur died on September 28, 1895, when he was seventy-two. He was surrounded by family, colleagues, and students. For nearly half a century, he had dominated the scientific world. For a quarter of a century, Pasteur had continued to do research despite his paralysis.

Pasteur's Legacy

The young men Pasteur had trained went on to make discoveries of their own. Dr. Roux and Dr. Yersin developed treatments for diphtheria, a disease that once killed thousands of children every year. Metchnikov, one of Pasteur's most brilliant assistants, began to uncover ways in which the body develops a resistance to microbes and develops immunities. Dr. Yersin also discovered the microbe that causes the plague.

It is tempting to talk about Pasteur as the genius who did it all. On the other hand, one might argue that if Pasteur hadn't made the discoveries, someone else would have. The truth is that nothing is achieved by one single effort. Scientists draw on the accumulation of knowledge brought about by many. In this way, it was possible for Pasteur to push forward the frontiers of science.

Most scientists acknowledge the importance of Pasteur's fierce determination to bring about scientific changes. What, for example, would have happened if other scientists, like Joseph Lister, had not recognized the truths Pasteur had uncovered?

Pasteur had once said to his students, "You bring me the deepest joy that can be felt by a man whose invincible belief it is that science and peace will triumph over ignorance and war...that the future will belong to those who will have done most for suffering humanity."

As he lay dying, Pasteur spoke his last words to his wife as she offered him a drink. "I can't," he said. These words ring with a sad irony, having been spoken by a man who never once entertained that idea in his life.

Joseph Lister greeting Louis Pasteur at the celebrations for his seventieth birthday at the Sorbonne. Pasteur is leaning on the arm of the President of the French Republic.

. . . .

"You have raised the veil that for all the centuries made infectious illness a dark mystery."

Joseph Lister, to Louis Pasteur, at his Jubilee

. . . .

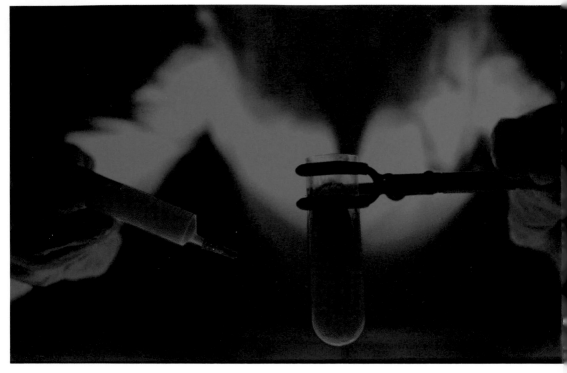

A recent experiment at the Pasteur Institute, a center for the study of microbes and microbial diseases. Microbial research at the institute has led to routine vaccines for polio, diphtheria, tetanus, measles, as well as vaccines for the epidemic diseases of typhoid, tuberculosis, and cholera. The AIDS virus was discovered there as well.

Modern Medicine

"Young people, trust scientific method, whose first secrets we yet scarcely know. Don't be discouraged. Live in the serene peace of laboratories and libraries. At the end of your life be able to say: I have done what I could."

Pasteur, to the young scientists of the Institute

Compared with the centuries of inexplicable disease that had gone before, events moved very swiftly following Pasteur's pioneering work against microbial disease in the 1870s and 1880s. By the end of the century, most of the bacteria that caused common diseases had been identified, many of them in Pasteur's laboratory in France and in the laboratories of Robert Koch in Germany.

By the turn of the century, people could be protected against several epidemic diseases, and there were antidotes to the bacterial poisons or toxins of diphtheria and tetanus. (The diphtheria toxin had been isolated by Roux and Yersin in 1888 at the Pasteur Institute, and the tetanus toxin, by scientists in Robert Koch's laboratory in 1890.)

In the twentieth century, effective vaccines have been developed against smallpox, tuberculosis, yellow fever, rabies, poliomyelitis, cholera, measles, typhoid, whooping cough, rubella, and influenza.

The major leap of the twentieth century has been the development of the drugs called antibiotics that can destroy infection in the body without harming the person.

After the first use of penicillin in 1941, other antibiotics were swiftly developed, a fitting culmination to the hundred years since Louis Pasteur's first work on fermentation started the process of finding ways to control or eradicate disease.

"That enthusiasm which has possessed you from the outset, my dear collaborators—keep it, but let strict verification be its traveling companion. Never put forward an opinion which cannot be simply and decisively proved. Make a cult of the critical spirit. By itself it can neither awaken ideas nor spur the mind to great things. Without it, everything is frail and precarious. Invariably, it has the last word."

Pasteur, to the young scientists of the Institute

Glossary

Anthrax: A highly infectious disease of cattle and sheep that can be transmitted to humans.
Antiseptic: A substance that kills or inhibits the growth of disease-causing microorganisms, but essentially is not poisonous to the body.
Asepsis: The absence of germs and the way of achieving a germ-free condition in surgery.
Bacillus: [Plural: bacilli] Any rod-shaped bacterium.
Bacterium: [Plural: bacteria] Any one of a large group of single-celled microorganisms. They are mostly responsible for the decay of dead plants and animals.
Carbolic acid: A poisonous white acid, made from

petroleum, which is used as an antiseptic.
Cholera: A serious intestinal illness caused by drinking water containing the cholera microbe, which is transmitted by human or animal feces.
Chrysalis: The third stage in the life of a butterfly or moth. During this stage, the insect changes into the adult form.
Cocoon: A silky protective covering spun by a silkworm to protect its chrysalis.
Crystal: A structure with a regular shape, in which the sides intersect at regular angles.
Culture: The growing of microorganisms in a suitable medium under controlled conditions.
Diphtheria: A very infectious disease caused by a bacillus. Diphtheria often used to be

fatal in small children.
Dissymmetry: The relationship between two objects when one is the mirror image of the other.
Epidemic: The widespread occurrence of a disease.
Electron microscope: A microscope that uses a beam of electrons instead of light for magnification. It was first used in 1931.
Fermentation: A process of decomposition (rotting) brought about by microorganisms, especially bacteria and yeasts. Pasteur's work caused scientists to divide fermentation into three main areas: alcoholic in which alcohol is produced during wine or beer making; acetic in which wine and other alcohols are turned into vinegar; and

lactic in which the sugars in milk are turned into acids - for example when milk goes sour.

Germ: A microorganism; in popular terminology, a microbe.

Immunization: To protect against a disease, usually by inoculation.

Incubator: A box or oven that keeps its contents at a constant temperature.

Inoculation: To place a measured dose of modified bacillus or other disease-causing microbe into a human or animal in order to cause the body to produce its own defense against the disease. Also called vaccination.

Lactic acid: A syrupy acid found in sour milk and also in some types of fruit.

Maggot: The second (or larval) stage of flies; usually found in rotting substances like meat, after the adult fly has laid its eggs.

Microorganism: Any creature that is too small to be seen with the naked eye.

Microbe: A microorganism.

Microbiology: The study of microorganisms.

Pasteurization: A process, pioneered by Pasteur, of heating wine, beer, and other liquids to prevent harmful bacteria from ruining the fermentation. Also used on milk and other foods to destroy harmful bacteria.

Plague: Diseases that cause epidemics by being very infectious and causing deaths.

Pneumonia: An infection of the lungs. The lungs partly fill with liquid, so that the flooded areas cannot be used for breathing. Usually caused by a virus.

Prussia: Former German state located in north-central Europe.

Pus: A yellow-green fluid that appears in wounds infected by certain bacteria; a clear sign that the wound is not healing properly.

Rabies: An infectious disease of the nervous system of warm-blooded animals, caused by a virus. It is passed to humans by the bite of an infected animal. Symptoms include convulsions, excessive saliva production, and (in humans) an aversion to water. The disease is also known as hydrophobia.

Saliva: The liquid produced by glands in the mouth. Its purpose is to make it easier to swallow food.

Smallpox: A very infectious disease caused by a virus.

Although not always fatal, this disease was a major killer until well into the twentieth century. It is now eradicated from the world.

Solution: A liquid mixture of two atoms or molecules, where they blend completely.

Spontaneous generation: A discredited scientific theory, which held that, given the right conditions, life would appear without any cause.

Stroke: The breaking of a blood vessel in the brain. The result may be paralysis, loss of speech, and brain damage.

Sugar beet: A vegetable from whose large white roots sugar can be extracted.

Tuberculosis: An infectious disease caused by a bacillus that mainly attacks the lungs.

Typhoid fever: A very infectious disease, caught by eating or drinking something contaminated by the feces of someone infected with the bacillus.

Vaccination: *See Inoculation.*

Virus: A type of microorganism that can only reproduce within the body of another animal or human.

Yeast: A type of fungus used in the fermentation industries and in baking.

Important Dates

1822	**Dec 27:** Louis Pasteur is born in Dole, France.
1843	Pasteur enters the Ecole Normale in fourth place.
1848	Pasteur reads his paper on crystals to the Academy of Science.
1849	Pasteur is appointed Lecturer of Chemistry at Strasbourg University.
	May 29: Pasteur marries Marie Laurent.
1853	Pasteur is awarded the Legion d'Honneur. Daughter, Cecile, is born.

1854	Pasteur, aged only thirty-one, is made Professor of Chemistry and Dean of the new Faculty of Science at Lille.
1855	Pasteur begins studies on fermentation.
1856	Pasteur becomes Director of Scientific Studies at the Ecole Normale.
1859	Their oldest daughter, Jeanne, dies from typhoid fever at age nine. Pasteur begins studies into spontaneous generation.
1862	Pasteur is elected to the Academy of Science.
1864	**Apr:** Pasteur demonstrates his germ theory at the Sorbonne in Paris.
	July: Pasteur goes to Arbois to test the wine fermentation. He discovers that heating the wine to 122-140 degrees Fahrenheit, (50-60 degrees Celsius) will prevent it going acid; he invents pasteurization.
1865	**June:** Pasteur goes to Alais in southern France to investigate a disease that is killing the silkworms. His father dies suddenly.
	Sept: His two-year old daughter, Camille, dies from typhoid fever.
1866	**May:** Twelve-year-old Cecile dies from typhoid fever.
1867	**May:** Pasteur is awarded a Grand Prize medal at the Exposition Universelle for his work on pasteurization. He is appointed Professor of Chemistry at the Sorbonne in Paris.
1868	**Oct 19:** Pasteur has a stroke. He is forty-five.
1869	The Franco-Prussian war starts.
1870	Pasteur starts studying beer fermentation.
1873	Pasteur elected to the Academy of Medicine.
1876	Pasteur publishes his "Studies on Beer."
1877	Pasteur starts studying anthrax after an outbreak in eastern France.
1879	During work on chicken cholera, Pasteur discovers how to immunize against disease using weakened microbes.
1880	Pasteur starts studying the disease of rabies.
1881	**June 5:** Pasteur's anthrax vaccine is a complete success. He is awarded the Grand Cross of the Legion d'Honneur.
1885	**July 6:** Joseph Meister is brought to Pasteur, having been bitten by a rabid dog. Pasteur decides to vaccinate him, the first person ever to be vaccinated against rabies. He survives and patients come from all over France for treatment.
1888	**Nov 14:** The Pasteur Institute is officially opened.
1892	**Dec 27:** A great ceremony is held at the Sorbonne to recognize Pasteur's achievements.
1893	The Pasteur Institute achieves a vaccination for diphtheria.
1894	**Sept 28:** Pasteur dies at Villeneuve L'Etang, aged seventy-two.

For More Information

Books

Birch, Beverley. *Pasteur's Fight Against Microbes* (Science Stories). Hauppauge, NY: Barrons Juveniles, 1996.

Jakab, E.A.M. A. *Louis Pasteur: Hunting Killer Germs*. New York, NY: McGraw-Hill Companies, 1999.

Sabin, Francene. *Louis Pasteur: Young Scientist*. Mahwah, NJ: Troll Communications LLC, 1997.

Smith, Linda Wasmer. *Louis Pasteur: Disease Fighter* (Great Minds of Science). Springfield, NJ: Enslow Publishers, Inc., 1997.

Web site

The Pasteur Institute

Learn more about Louis Pasteur and the Pasteur Institute, which he founded in 1887—www.pasteur.fr/pasteur/presentation/IP.html.

Index